A 9-11 Confession:
10 years in the Making

The Journey of a
Disaster Mental Health Worker

A 9-11 Confession:
10 years in the Making

The Journey of a
Disaster Mental Health Worker

Copyright © 2011
Maureen A. McInnis, MS, LCPC
1 Gypsy Press, pllc

A 9-11 Confession: 10 years in the Making.
The Journey of a Disaster Mental Health Worker

Copyright © 2011 by Maureen A. McInnis, MS, LCPC
All rights reserved

Published by 1 Gypsy Press, pllc
Great Falls, Montana

For information, address:
1 Gypsy Press, pllc,
1601 2nd Ave North, Suite 200, Great Falls, MT 59401
(406-452-1171)

Cover Design by Rhonda Kueffler,
Copyright belongs to 1 Gypsy Press, pllc

ISBN-13: 978-0-9838566-0-3

ISBN-10: 0983856605

Printed in the United States of America

Dedicated to:

The families and individuals who on
September 11, 2001
lost a loved one
were physically harmed
or emotionally affected
by this terrorist attack.

May we never forget.

Acknowledgements

THANK YOU,

First to my husband Don, who encouraged and supported this project and my wondering off to other places without him so I could volunteer.

Second, a special thanks to Penny Thomas, from **Direct Response Copy that Opens Wallets,** PennyThomas.com. Without her assistance and hard work this book would still be in my head and not in your hands.

To Rhonda Kueffler, for her professional graphic art talent.

To Don, Julie, and David for pre-reading my book. They laughed, they cried, they made corrections.

To the American Red Cross for giving me the opportunity to have this experience.

To every family and volunteer I met on this adventure.

Table of Contents

0

Chapter One

Getting the Call

"Where were you when the world stopped turning on that September day?"
Alan Jackson
October 2001

Some of us can remember where we were when we heard of John F. Kennedy's assassination. Or when the Challenger shuttle exploded. Or the horrific death of Princess Diana. Big events have a way of freezing time in our minds.

Where were you when the world stopped turning on that September day?

Breaking News

Ten years ago I was at a professional seminar at a local hotel in Great Falls, Montana, a long way from New York City, on that September day. Oblivious to any world changing news, I stood outside the seminar room entrance waiting for my friend Greg. I watched as he crossed the calm, cool courtyard decorated in New Orleans, Bourbon Street décor.

Without even saying hello, he blurted out, "Have you seen the news?"

"No," I answered. A long time ago I learned that I'm a news junkie, so watching TV in the morning makes me late.

"Two planes crashed into the Twin Towers."

"What?" I could barely grasp what he was saying.

"The World Trade Center in New York was hit by two airplanes; they think it might be a terrorist attack."

It took a little while for this to completely sink in. The enormity of this disaster was going to be difficult to comprehend and overwhelming.

When it finally did sink in, I knew I needed to call the Red Cross.

In a very selfish way, I knew that this was a big moment in history and I wanted to be a part of it. I wanted to go to New York City and be a part of something that would forever be in our history books. I wanted to say that I was there.

But first, I needed to get through this morning. I was already at the seminar and needed to complete that first. I really couldn't do anything at that moment anyway.

It was hard to concentrate on anything, much less a repetitive presentation of 'Cognitive Behavioral Therapy.'

During the break, most everyone at the seminar went to the hotel lounge to hear more about what happened. All eyes and ears were glued to the TV for more information about the morning event in New York City.

We watched the videos play again and again as the buildings collapsed into a mushroom cloud of debris and human life.

It was a clear day in New York City, bright blue skies without a cloud to be seen above. I heard on a later newscast that one airline pilot said, "It was too perfect a day," referring to the weather.

Volunteering

During my lunch break, I decided to head straight home to call the American Red Cross and offer to volunteer. They had already beaten me to it. They had already called and left a message wanting to know if I was available and when.

They were reaching out for volunteers and possible dates of availability.

I called them right back.

How do you say NO to an event like this?

As I noted earlier, I needed to make this trip. I needed to be a part of this event. To put into action my crisis training. I felt I needed to go and experience this tragedy for myself.

This was the kind of mental health counseling I liked doing, even if it meant putting on hold my clients, my practice and my life.

This was the mental health counseling I thrived on and the American Red Cross Disaster Mental Health Program was just the place for me to do it.

Volunteering comes naturally to me. If I could live off volunteering, I would do it more often.

My father was a small rural medical doctor, a general practitioner. On his days off, he ran a free medical clinic at the Catholic Mission on the Indian Reservation north of the small town where I grew up. Some days he would put four or five dollars in the free offering basket at the Mission, and at the end of the day it would only have 30 or 40 cents in it.

I remember his last Christmas with us. He made a house call to an elderly gentleman who probably had no more than a cold. I caught him returning home.

"Dad, you shouldn't be making house calls on Christmas Day. You should be here with us." I remember saying.

"Did you know I was gone?" asked my father

"No," was the only truthful answer I could give him.

"I spent thirty minutes with a lonely old man on Christmas Day. That most likely made his day. You've had me for almost two days and didn't even know I was gone. Think about that Maureen," he said in return.

I understood him completely at that moment.

My father often saw people at no charge, or a whole family for the cost of one office call.

I remember a farmer who harvested and boiled maple syrup. He gave my father a gallon of maple syrup in exchange for the house call he made that day to his country farm.

My father often gave away his expertise and good medicine.

My mother was her own force in volunteerism.

She was on the local school board for 14 years or more. Mom was very active in our local Girl Scout units as well as the Girl Scout Council. She also volunteered for the local Catholic Church. It was more like she volunteered us kids for the local church.

With her kids grown and gone, my mother still volunteers at the local library. She doesn't miss her appointed time, unless she's out of town or there's too much snow for her to drive in comfortably.

As you can see, volunteering comes naturally for me.

So I had to volunteer for this event. I just felt this was where I needed to be.

The American Red Cross

I have been an American Red Cross volunteer on and off throughout my life. I gave blood, taught First Aid, CPR and water safety courses. In time I allowed my volunteerism to slip away.

So when I read an article in the American Counseling Association's monthly publication about a volunteer opportunity for mental health counselors I took advantage of the opportunity. The American Red Cross was looking for professionals who they would train in Disaster Mental Health Issues and the Red Cross procedures. In exchange they asked for two-week commitments.

I saw it as an opportunity to do pure mental health counseling - no notes, no billing, just meeting people at their level and helping them get their needs meet.

I chose to get the training and then dedicate two weeks of each year to the American Red Cross as a Disaster Mental Health Worker. In the summer of 2000, I worked the forest fires in Montana, just 250 miles from home. Over the Fourth of July period of 2001 I had gone to Houston, Texas to help out after Tropical Storm Allison caused a great deal of flooding.

When I returned home from Houston I had my own minor crisis to deal with. While I was gone, my father-in-law became seriously ill. He died the morning after I returned. I was thankful I was able to see him one last time. By the time the funeral and burial were over, I had been away from my practice and clients for over three weeks at the beginning of the summer in 2001.

So when that fateful September day happened, I had already used up my two-week self-imposed commitment to the Red Cross. Yet I still felt compelled to travel to New York. I told the Red Cross

I could be available on October 1st. I then started preparing my clients for my second long absence.

Preparation

After I hung up with the Red Cross, I asked myself, *how do you prepare for this type of disaster?* The disasters I knew and trained for were natural ones - flood, hurricane, tornado, and forest or home fires.

The destruction of the Twin Towers was not a natural disaster - it was intentional. This was an act of terrorism on American soil. And, with the exception of the Oklahoma City bombing, we had never been attacked on our own soil by terrorists. The damage and aftermath of this kind of attack would need a different kind of counseling mindset.

The size of the destruction was what overwhelmed me.

I live in Great Falls, Montana, population 50,000 plus. Our tallest building is nine-stories high. We have another three or four that might be six or seven stories high. The downtown area averages between two or four stories. The town I grew up in had a population of only 1200 people.

The Twin Towers stood 110 stories high, each. The enormity of the buildings that collapsed and the number of people potentially harmed was just overwhelming.

Although crisis work has always come easy to me, I wasn't sure how to make sense of this. If I couldn't make sense of it, how was I going to help the people in New York make sense of it?

I am a natural researcher, so I started studying about disaster counseling. I learned a lot about trauma, post-traumatic stress disorder and critical incident debriefing.

This began a whole new learning process that would help me prepare for my trip to Ground Zero. I was beginning to understand how to make sense out of this crisis.

Chapter Two

Leaving and Arriving

Three weeks after the day *'the world stopped turning'* I was on the first leg of my journey to New York and the 9-11 crisis.

My Red Cross assignment turned out to be in Newark, New Jersey. This was determined in a roundabout way. Since I had called three weeks earlier, the assumption was I would be going to New York City itself. The Red Cross originally told me I was to go to New York, JFK airport and to report to Pier 94, where they had their Service Center.

This plan changed when a New Jersey Family Assistance Center opened up. I then had instructions to fly into LaGuardia Airport. I did not realize that meant finding my own way across the East River, through Manhattan, across the Hudson River and into New Jersey. I was not very comfortable with this, as I am known for getting lost.

Two days before my scheduled departure, they changed my destination yet again – this time to New Jersey - Newark Airport. I would then report to the Family Service Center at an old train terminal in Liberty State Park called the Central Railroad of New Jersey Terminal. I was a little happier with this plan as it involved having to navigate in a much smaller geographic area.

Leaving

October 1st finally arrived – I was packed and ready to go on my mission and adventure. My initial flight into Salt Lake City departed at 6:30 in the morning. In the past couple of weeks' the authorities had put in place an order that all passengers needed to show up two hours before their flight for security reasons.

Now I am one to follow orders. The airport is near where my husband worked, so I got him to drop me off on his way in to work. That happened to be 3:50 a.m. Well, Great Falls, Montana International Airport wasn't open at that time of the morning, so I had to wait outside for forty minutes in the cold morning air. Something told me this was going to be a long day.

The plane change in Salt Lake City went smoothly – next stop Newark, New Jersey. I spent the long flight thinking about what lay ahead. I had worked out a couple of different scenarios in my head. I wanted to be prepared for whatever would come my way.

If I can preplan scenarios in my head, I feel like I am better prepared for any crisis I might run into. It also helps me mask my reaction when I'm more fascinated by what's going on, or so shocked that I don't want to look surprised or out of control. This is my coping mechanism.

Apparently, I was so engrossed in building a storehouse of possible scenarios I missed the approach to Newark Airport. I surprisingly didn't look out of the plane window to see New York City and Ground Zero as we came in for our landing.

Arriving

To me the Newark Airport was huge; however, the large overhead direction boards made it possible to successfully and efficiently find the baggage carousel. Unfortunately, my luggage didn't find its way there successfully or efficiently. I happened to notice that neither did the luggage of four other passengers on that flight. I also noticed that all four of those people had sat in the same row as I did. The Delta representative told us our luggage was 'delayed indefinitely!'

Fortunately for us, our luggage popped up on the carousel about twenty minutes later.

It made me wonder if our row was tagged with suspicion. My flight was changed suddenly two days ago. The couple on in the other half of the row looked Oriental. I don't remember what the man at the end of my row looked like.

When I landed in Newark my instructions were to catch the AirTrain – an elevated monorail that runs between the airport terminals, parking lots and NJ Transit train station – to Station P4 to get the hotel shuttle bus. Sounded easy enough, but first I had to find the AirTrain.

Terminal B was crawling with New Jersey National Guard personnel so I asked one for directions. You would have thought he would know where the train station was. But no, this young man was new to the airport and did not know how to help me. After walking around a bit I finally found the AirTrain, tucked away in a corner out of sight!

With the AirTrain ride successfully accomplished, my next search was for the hotel shuttle.

I found the shuttle and Adam.

Adam was an AmeriCorps worker, who was waiting for the same shuttle bus.

AmeriCorps workers are college students doing volunteer work for the experience and money toward college. I love these young people. I worked with several of them while I was in Texas. They have energy, a new perspective, and enough mischief to remind you of when you were once young.

Adam was wonderful. He came from a Red Cross office in Indiana. He was very energetic.

Adam was good at introducing himself first and then helping other people to meet each other. He introduced himself first to me then to the driver. Then he introduced the driver to me. The driver had a helper for the luggage, so Adam introduced himself to the helper, and then introduced the helper to me. We were the only two passengers on the bus and Adam talked all the way to the hotel. I found Adam to be delightful and I hoped I would be able to see more of him.

Finally – At the Hotel

After checking in at the hotel, Adam disappeared. He said he needed to make more phone calls. He had to tell everyone back home what was going on.

It was now getting late in the evening and I was hungry, so I came back to the lobby looking for a place to eat. They didn't have a restaurant, but the next hotel over did.

In the lobby, I met a woman who was a nurse by profession and had come from Kodiak, Alaska. Her journey had been far longer than mine had. She left her little island and flew first to Anchorage. She then flew overnight into Seattle, arriving early in the morning. From there she flew to Newark. Over dinner, we talked about our expectations and concerns. We had a nice dinner. After we checked in at the Red Cross Administrative Center, I did not see her again until the day before we left.

The next morning I met with the Red Cross and AmeriCorps volunteers over a continental breakfast in the hotel lobby area. That day's focus was to get to the Red Cross Administrative Center to check in and find out what our assignments would be.

Adam, bless his heart, was seated next to the breakfast room door and greeted everyone who came in. At one point he said, "Oh this is just like the *Amazing Race*, and we're all waiting for our next clue so we know where to go for our next destination!"

American Red Cross, New Jersey

Three vans pulled up outside the hotel. Upwards of twenty-one volunteers and their luggage crammed in for the ride to a college campus somewhere in New Jersey. This was where the Red Cross had set up their Central Administrative Center.

The Red Cross had set up in a series of college classrooms. I dropped off my luggage in the assigned area. I then went through a series of six check-in stations: Health, Travel, Finances, Car, Location Assignment, and Lodgings. This took the better part of the day. I briefly saw Adam before he left for his assignment. He said that he was going to some kind of centralized service area where they have resources to help families find their relatives. I wished him well.

14

I was assigned a car and handed a set of car keys. I was told the make and license number of the car and a vague description where it was in the college parking lot. It took me fifteen minutes to find it.

I was told that as I was a day early, I was going to spend one day and one evening with the Port Authority of New York and New Jersey Central at the Marriott Hotel, back at Newark Airport.

Getting Lost – Part One

The trip from the college campus to the Marriott Hotel at Newark Airport was a nightmare. Apparently I just don't 'get' airports with their circular road system and over and underpasses and loops. I went around and around the airport a few times and seemed to come back to the same wrong place.

Finally, I stopped at a taxi stand and jumped out of the car to ask for directions. One taxi driver, bless his heart, seeing that I was with the American Red Cross, helped me out. He said, "Just stay to the left and keep taking the left exit." I eventually got to the Marriott before darkness took over.

The World Trade Center was owned by The Port Authority of New York and New Jersey, and many of their employees were impacted by the destruction of the Twin Towers. They had set up their temporary headquarters at the Marriott Hotel. This site offered its employees a one-stop location where they could check in with personnel, insurance

15

adjustors, sign-up for the bus ride to the memorial service, and receive services offered by the American Red Cross – like mental health services.

On October 3rd, a memorial service for the victims of the World Trade Center Towers collapse was going to be held at Madison Square Garden. The Port Authority chartered buses to the service and people had been coming in for days to register for the Memorial Service and bus ride. There were three or four mental health workers available to assist. The other mental health workers had been there for several days and would accompany the families to the Memorial Service. My assignment was to remain at the Hotel and be available to any stragglers who came and wanted help, or just to talk.

My Work Begins –
The Port Authority Worker

My first interaction came early the morning of the Memorial Service. I met with a Port Authority worker who had safely evacuated from one of the Towers. He was struggling with claustrophobia and was having difficulty being indoors and trying to do his job.

His work department had been relocated to a hangar at the JFK Airport. Even with all that space, he was still uncomfortable being indoors; he felt overwhelmed and struggled to be himself again.

I asked him to tell me his story of the planes hitting the Towers.

He said that the only thing he really remembered about that Tuesday was looking up and out of the window. In front of him he could see the tail of the first plane hit the Towers.

When the plane hit, he was surprised how calm he felt. Even though he knew this was an emergency, he was still feeling in control of himself.

He started to calmly and quickly gather people and direct them to leave the office through the emergency stairs. He could smell the airplane fuel so he believed that a fire would be coming next.

He then told me a second story. When he served in the Navy, there had been a fire onboard his ship while they were at sea. He continued telling me that when you have a fire onboard a ship, you go <u>up</u> the stairs. But when you have a fire in a building, you go <u>down</u> the stairs.

Still completely in control, he went into the stairwell with the others. When he got into the dark smoky stairwell, all he could remember was feeling like he was back on the burning ship and he needed to get topside. So up the stairs he started to climb. He believes the people going down the stairs grabbed him and pulled him down with them. He really didn't remember.

He then told me that the next time he became conscious of his environment was about two weeks later while working in his garden. He noted to himself how impressed he was by how neat and clean the garden was. He figured he must have been out working in the garden for those two weeks without knowing for sure where he was or what he was doing.

The last thing he remembered was stepping into the dark and smoky stairwell, and going up the stairs trying to get topside on his Navy ship.

We talked about the ship fire for a little bit. As I listened to him, I could sense Post-Traumatic Stress Disorder (PTSD). One of the things I had learned in my research before this trip was that a previous experience can become a flashback and can get mixed up in a current disaster.

I got him hooked up with the Veterans Service near where he lived in New Jersey. He promised me that he would go because it was important to him. Then as we were ending our talk, he wanted to know where I was from. When I told him Montana, he was quite delighted. He had ridden his Harley-Davidson through much of the West. He rode mostly on the back roads and state highways. He said he loved Montana with all its wide, open spaces. Going there was a great experience for him.

He left feeling much better and with a better understanding of what might have happened to him. Although I was never able to follow up on him, I really enjoyed meeting him and helping him find the support he needed, not only for the current traumatic event, but hooking him up with services he could have used many years before.

Downtime

The rest of that day was very quiet. I talked casually with the Port Authority officers and ran errands for the other Red Cross workers.

My assignment that evening was to wait at the Marriott while the other Red Cross workers accompanied families to the memorial service, which was held at Madison Square Garden.

Posted in the same area that the Red Cross workers we had set up their tables were tripods with page after page from the *New York Times*, dedicated to the individuals lost in the Twin Towers collapse. Column after column, six or seven inches in length, told the stories of the missing persons. Some had pictures, some didn't.

One story talked about having a fight before they left for work that morning and not having the opportunity to make up.

One family talked about the father who coached their ball team and what that involvement meant to them as a family and to the child being coached.

Many of the stories spoke of things they said or wished they had said that morning, or the family's traditional morning routines.

All the articles ended in how much they missed their loved ones.

I talked briefly to a woman who had signed up for the bus ride to the Memorial Service. She had lost a family member who worked for the Port Authority.

She had been taking advantage of the help from the disaster mental health workers. She was glad for the opportunity to go to the Memorial Service without having to make the drive herself.

The Insurance Adjuster

After the buses returned and the families had left to go home, the workers staying at the Marriott met in the lounge to unwind.

Among the workers, I noticed a rather disturbed young man. He was lighting up one cigarette after another, drinking one beer after another. It appeared as though he couldn't drink enough or smoke enough to forget everything that was going on in his head.

A Red Cross Disaster Mental Health Worker is never really off duty, so I thought I'd talk to him to see how he was doing.

This young man, only 20 or 22 years old, worked for the insurance company that the Port Authority had their insurance through. He was still dressed in his suit and tie. He talked to me about how hard it was to listen to all the stories - stories of people and their experience of panic and having to leave the building without really understanding what was going on. Family members who were trying to make sense out of what happened and why couldn't they find their loved one?

He shared a couple of stories he'd heard. One story had really left him disturbed involved a longtime maintenance worker at the World Trade Center who was also there in 1993 when the first bombing happened in the underground parking lot. This man still worked at the World Trade Center when the planes hit and the Towers fell. He was confused and overwhelmed by it all. He was still struggling to understand and make sense of what happened.

There were many similar stories of fear and panic told to this young man. He was not prepared to hear the repeated trauma that each policyholder was required to share with him. He may have had the skills to process insurance claims, but he was not trained or qualified to deal with the emotional side of his assignment.

He shared with me that he had gone home over the previous weekend. He went out with all his young friends and listened to them complain about petty items. They talked on and on about who liked who and who was talking about whom. He found it to be immature and actually annoying to be around.

He found that he couldn't even be near his own friends. That listening every day to people whose lives were devastated by the Towers being destroyed was more important and pertinent than the insignificant banter of whether somebody liked them or called them a name, or some of that petty stuff that young people talk about.

I could see that he was detaching himself more and more, not only from his friends and family, but also from life. What I also know is that you cannot counsel drunks. All I could do was listen to him.

I did know that this assignment was far too emotional and stressful for one person to do without additional support and help. This young man had been doing this assignment for almost three weeks without friends, family, or fellow insurance workers. He was doing it all alone.

The next day I talked to the other Red Cross workers in order to find someone to help him. I told them of my experience with him the night before and wanted them to check in on him and make sure that he could get some help. I couldn't stay because I needed to be at my next assignment - The Family Assistance Center located at the Central Railroad of New Jersey Terminal in Liberty State Park.

I still think of him. What I really fear is he isn't alive. I feel that suicide may have been the only way to stop all the stories that were consuming him. I often wonder if his company fired him because he turned out to be an incompetent employee due to that experience. Or I wonder if he turned into an alcoholic and was incapable of doing his job.

Was the insurance company able to recognize that the job they assigned him was destroying him? Wherever he is, he is certainly in my prayers and thoughts because I do think of him often.

He was a victim of the 9-11 tragedy by proxy. He had no direct connections to New York or the World Trade Center, but he listened every day for three weeks to the stories of victims and family members. It started to consume and overtake him. He was not the typical person we were looking to help in that tragedy; he was, however, very much a victim, if only a silent one.

This may have been the end of one assignment, but it was the beginning of my real journey. The journey that will stay with me the rest of my life.

Chapter Three

Central Railroad of New Jersey Terminal Liberty State Park

Getting Lost – Part Two

After getting lost driving from the Red Cross Administrative Center to the Marriott Hotel at Newark Airport, I decided to recruit a Port Authority worker to escort me to my next assignment – The New Jersey Family Assistance Center at the Central Railroad of New Jersey Terminal in Liberty State Park.

The instructions looked easy. Take the highway to Exit A, 'Liberty State Park', and then follow the brick road to the Railroad Terminal. When

I got to Exit A, I was confident I could make it the rest of the way alone, so I waved off my escort and turned off the highway. Even though I was following him, he ignored my wave-off, slowed down, swerved to take the exit and followed me down the ramp to save me from getting lost again.

He did this because he had noticed the detour sign saying "Family Assistance Center, Exit C." I was so busy trying not to get lost that I didn't even see the 'flashing' traffic billboard. So I was lost again. This time I just followed the Port Authority worker through Liberty State Park.

Lady Liberty

The detour turned out to be a lucky mistake on my part. As I obediently followed my escort through the Park, I wondered if I would catch sight of the Statue of Liberty. And then I saw her, straight ahead.

I was surprised how big she was. I'm not sure what I was expecting, but there she was, tall and green against that deep blue sky. I was so engrossed by what I was seeing, I failed to notice that the road had taken a gentle turn to the left and I ran off the road.

Fortunately, I was inside the Park so I drove off onto the grass. This was just as good a time to stop and get a really good look at her. What a magnificent symbol of America's liberty, freedom, and acceptance of foreign citizens.

What a contrast to the site just across the river.

I wasn't allowed to have a camera, so I had to imprint this vision in my mind. I was told before I left that cameras or any picture taking were not going to be allowed on this assignment. Breaking this rule was grounds to be sent home.

So I just stood there and soaked up the view.

The View Across the Hudson

I got back in my car, steered it back on to the road, and continued to follow my helpful and patient Port Authority escort. We drove to the northern end of Liberty State Park where the Central Railroad of New Jersey Terminal was located.

It took a while for me to find a parking place. I found one at the far end of the parking lot. Walking up to the Railroad Terminal I was looking straight across the Hudson River at New York City. My escort wanted to see what was going on and have a good look too, so he walked with me.

I had to ask my escort where the World Trade Center Towers had been. He pointed straight across and said, "There, right between the two green-roofed buildings...where the smoke is rising." And yes, I could see, even now, more than three weeks after the event, the smoke was still rising.

With or without the Towers, it was quite a view. We were directly across the Hudson from lower Manhattan. When I got closer to the Railroad

27

Terminal, I looked to my right and saw Ellis Island. Beyond Ellis Island, I could see the Statue of Liberty again.

I was standing at the Gateway to America.

The Terminal

The Central Railroad of New Jersey Terminal was built in 1889. It was the largest transportation facility at the turn of the century. The building jointly served as a bus, train and ferry terminal. Between the years 1890 and 1915, the Terminal saw 30,000 to 50,000 people pass through its doors daily. At its peak, in 1929, 21 million passengers passed through its doors, getting on and off one of the 300 daily trains, changing buses, or catching one of the 128 daily ferries to New York City.

It stopped functioning as a transport center in 1967 and fell into disrepair. In 1975, it was listed in the National Register of Historical Places. It also became a part of the 1,222-acre Liberty State Park. The Park was opened and dedicated on Flag Day - June 14, 1976. The Terminal is now restored and is open to the public.

This historical site was selected at the request of Diane DiFrancesco, New Jersey's First Lady. She wanted to provide a Family Assistance Center for the victims of September 11 in New Jersey. Her reasoning was that a large majority of individuals who passed through the World Trade Center lived in New Jersey. The survivors and families of the missing should have equivalent facilities to those provided in New York at Pier 94.

Rumor has it that in less than forty-eight hours after the order went out to create an Assistance Center, the Terminal got cleaned, stocked with tables, chairs, a bank of telephones, and three portable classrooms. The grounds were landscaped, with trees, flowers and grass sod. That was pretty impressive.

N.O.V.A. – the National Organization for Victims Advocates – was in charge of this program and they invited The Salvation Army, the American Red Cross, and other New Jersey State agencies to complete the Family Assistance Center. The Salvation Army provided the food and spiritual support. The American Red Cross created their regular Service Center, which provided physical and mental health assistance, financial support and community resources. The New Jersey State Agencies were there to help people replace lost licenses and certificates, get death certificates, and any other state mandated paperwork.

The main building, built in an eclectic Victoria-era styling stands, three stories high. Its roof is steep and high-pitched with dormer windows on the third floor. All held high by prominent archway windows below. A large metal clock tower is attached to the front of the building that overlooks the river. On the opposite end of the building is the huge train shed covering twelve forgotten train platforms and partial rails.

I found myself stopping and staring a lot. I understood large, tall and massive from living near the Rocky Mountain Front and Glacier National Park. And yet I found these tall office buildings to be continuously fascinating.

However, I wasn't here to gawk.

I pulled myself together and headed in the building itself.

Inside the Terminal

I was eager to start my assignment and find my fellow mental health volunteers. I turned towards the building and walked through the large open bay doors of the train shed. Inside this area the Salvation Army had set up a white event tent. This tent was being used as the eating area. It was filled with ten or more white plastic circular tables with seating for eight. This was where The Salvation Army served lunch and dinner to all the volunteers.

Across the shed stood a bank of doors leading into the main terminal waiting room. I headed over to the doors to find a place to check in and find the Red Cross workers. I stepped into the open waiting room and was immediately taken by how beautiful this building was.

English buff colored glazed brick covered the walls. Red iron trusses, with a starburst design, supported the ceiling three stories above. Straight ahead rose a huge staircase that led to a brick wall. I believe the bricks covered the windows looking over the Hudson River. A balcony ran around two sides of this cathedral-like room, supported by more red iron beams in a wheat design.

As I walked into the waiting room, I noticed on the left side of the large, open room were a bank of telephones that the State of New Jersey supplied for long-distance phone calls to friends and family. All around the open area were tables and chairs. In a few spots, small intimate conversational areas had been set up with couches and chairs. One area had a television – it stayed on all day. The American Red Cross medical area, staffed with volunteer nurses, was set up on one side of the staircase.

A children's activity center was located off to the right. I found it rather impressive. A volunteer was there to look after the children of survivors and victim's families while they took advantage of the services offered.

The arrangement was ingenious. It was all portable and easy to set up and take down. Combined together several of these three to four-foot high cabinets opened up to form a 15-foot by 30-foot corral to safely enclose the children.

These cabinets held all the items needed to equip a children's activity center – colorful mats, little tables and chairs, toys, arts and crafts supplies – all in tubs for easy set up and take-down. With their children safely playing and being entertained by a volunteer, parents could take care of their sad tasks.

The waiting room did not seem to have a place for me to report to, so I asked around. My directions were to head outside by way of the hallway to the right of the giant staircase, keep to the right and I would find the three portable classrooms where the American Red Cross Service Center was set up.

I walked to the back of the Terminal and out onto the river side of the building. As I rounded the corner to the courtyard of the portable classrooms, I could once again see across the river to Ground Zero, and to the right, Ellis Island and the Statue of Liberty.

Chapter Four

Meeting My Red Cross Team

When I rounded the corner, I came upon a tour for the volunteers. Several people were wearing American Red Cross vests, so I just followed them around.

I noticed one woman in particular who was wearing a Red Cross vest. After the tour, I introduced myself to her and asked if she knew where I should check in with the Red Cross. Since she had already checked in, she was more than happy to take me where I needed to go. She introduced herself and said that she was a Disaster Mental Health Worker. "Great!" I replied, "I'm also a Mental Health Worker."

Her name was Marti. She introduced me to the coordinator, who then sent the two of us off to meet up with two other Mental Health Workers. We found them wandering around the Train Terminal. We got together to talk in the large waiting area in one of the small conversations areas near the children's play area.

We were asked to pick a team leader. That individual would attend all the daily briefings and pass out any necessary information. The team leader also would be the one who would run interference with any questions. The team asked me to be in that position. Mostly because no one else wanted the responsibility.

In order to do Disaster Mental Health work with the American Red Cross, you have to be a licensed social worker or counselor in your own state and carry the necessary liability insurance. The Red Cross offers their specific training at National Conferences.

I am a professional counselor, licensed by the State of Montana, and the other three were licensed social workers.

Let me introduce you to them...

My Team

Rita was originally from New Jersey, but now lived and worked in Oregon as a social worker. While living in Oregon, or at least away from New Jersey, she had managed to lose her Jersey accent. However, as the days passed, she slipped back into it as seamlessly as she fit back into the New Jersey scene.

Rita and her native accent made it very easy for her to just start talking to people and make a connection. She was meeting people every day who knew the same communities and events that she did.

One evening we were having dinner together in an Italian restaurant at the Secaucus Mall. Our waitress came over to the table to take our order. Rita happened to notice that her pen was topped with a tiny Statue of Liberty. She started talking to the waitress about her being a former New Jersey girl and how much she missed seeing the Statue of Liberty every day. Without missing a beat, the waitress just handed her the pen. She said she could get another pen at a later date.

Rita was thrilled by the gift.

Dora was a licensed social worker from Florida, where she currently lived. She was originally from New York City or close by. She had spent a lot of time in New York City and knew it well. Dora was a true social worker. She just naturally loved talking to people and asking those, 'How can I help you?' questions.

She was fearless in asking around and finding resources to help those in need. She could easily speak up on other people's behalf.

Dora was the one who came upon a group of people who had been traumatized by the events of September 11th, but had not spoken to anybody about it. Only Dora, in her very special way, thought of talking to them.

They were the janitorial/maintenance crew at the Central Railroad of New Jersey Terminal. On that fateful September morning they were taking their cigarette break. Four or five of them were standing away from the terminal in front of the railing that overlooks the Hudson River across from Manhattan. It was the same location I stood at when I first arrived at the Family Assistance Center.

They were enjoying their break and commenting on how beautiful the day was. Then they heard a loud noise come from behind them. When they turned around to investigate, they saw a low-flying plane coming from the north. It appeared to be very low in the sky and picking up speed.

Each noted that this was an unusual sight because airspace was restricted in this area. The noise got louder and louder. It did not seem as though the plane was aware that it was flying too low or too fast.

They stood there in shock as they watched this plane fly down Manhattan and hit the North Tower.

They were not only witnesses to this historical tragedy, but were probably some of the few people who witnessed the first plane hit the Towers.

Dora was the first person in three weeks to talk to them or even ask how they were doing. In Dora's social worker way, she just asked the first worker she saw, "How are you doing?" That worker was so impressed with Dora that he brought a second worker to her the next time he saw her.

By the end of that day, she had talked to the four or five of the janitorial/ maintenance workers who were on that cigarette break and witnessed the airplane hitting that first Tower. Every day when she came to the Terminal, she checked in with them. I know they were very appreciative because I would overhear them talking about it repeatedly.

Dora was a true social worker.

Marti, originally from Sothern California, was now a social worker in Washington State. Like the other two social workers, she effortlessly made connections with people. She easily flowed among the families that came and went through the rail terminal. Marti has turned out to be a great friend to this day.

Before September 11th, I had been through her community several times on my way to Seattle from Oregon. I lived in Oregon before I moved to Montana. I often thought her community would be a great place to live. Marti was surprised that I knew of her community and had actually been through it.

My job as the team leader was to attend the morning briefings and get instructions for the day and share them with my team. Our primary mission was escorting families of the missing and dead to Ground Zero. We were going there via ferry across the Hudson River. We called ourselves *The Boat People*.

We would then return with them to the Family Assistance Center. We would stay with them until they left to go home. Our jobs were to casually meet them, assess their status and help them with anything we could. When the ferries weren't running, we were to just wander around the terminal and talk to people.

The Red Cross had additional disaster mental health workers who stayed at the center and met with people when they asked for assistance. This group of mental health workers saw regular clients who would return often, or people who would just stop by once.

When the ferries were not running, we walked around and talked to the staff in the portable classrooms to see how they were holding up to the stress of the job. We met people who came to the Family Assistance Center to get help and directed or escorted them to the right services. We often just stopped and talked to whoever was around. Imagine that, an assignment in which you just talked and listen to people. This is my favorite part of being a volunteer disaster mental health worker.

There was an organization that brought a therapeutic dog to the Family Assistance Center. The dog, its handler and a Red Cross worker walked around talking to people. Therapy dogs have an uncanny ability to sense grief and give comfort to the griever.

In my wanderings around the Terminal, I came across people who were in different stages of grief and acceptance.

I spent a lot of my time around the memorial boards – these three-sided, six-foot high corkboards were in the train shed. People pinned up messages to loved ones, pictures, stories – whatever they wanted and felt they needed to do to help them with their grief.   I wanted to be there for the family members, the people who were directly affected by September 11th. I must have read every board twice if not more. I needed to absorb what happened through their eyes and their words.

The Sister

There was a young lady who came every afternoon to the memorial boards after she was done with work. She had started with a poster asking if anyone had seen her sister. The poster had her sister's picture and an upbeat description of her and where her office was in the Tower. The first day she came, it was just a plain poster. The next day she edged it with crepe paper. She was framing the poster to help it stand out. As if making the poster easier to read or see would bring her sister back. On the last day of my assignment, I saw her add even more things to the poster so people would really notice it.

Her sister was working on the 90th floor of one of the towers. 'Please' she wrote, 'have you seen my sister?' The first day I saw her, I stopped to talk to her. She said she didn't want to talk. Actually, she never wanted to talk. She just wanted her sister. I came by every day about that same time looking for her. I would hang around hoping to be helpful. I never spoke to her again, and she never spoke to me. I just honored her request.

Mother and the Newlyweds

Another day I noticed a family of three attaching a picture to one of the boards. I walked over and introduced myself. I asked if they had a family member in the Towers when they collapsed. They did.

The wife had lost her husband. The son had lost his father. The third woman was the son's bride of 1 month. Only the son spoke.

About a year ago, his father had developed a severe case of depression. He struggled with his illness and was up and down for months. He had even spent some time in a hospital. For awhile it appeared he might not recover from the depression or return to work. The family was very worried about him. However, with time, medication and professional help he was able to recover. In early August of 2001, he was finally ready and able to return to work.

This was a great relief to the son because he was going to be wed that fall. The wedding was scheduled the weekend before September 11th. The son said that it was such a joyous weekend. His father was feeling better and appeared to really enjoy the wedding. He was happy for his mother that her husband had recovered.

The son said that his wedding was a welcome event after a long and difficult year dealing with his father's depression. The wedding turned out to be an excellent way to conclude a difficult year for his mother and celebrate his father's return to full-time work.

He and his bride left that next day, Sunday, for their honeymoon in the Caribbean. On that Tuesday morning his mother called him to tell him about the two planes that hit the World Trade Center's Twin Towers. Could he please come home?

His father worked in one of the Towers and was killed in the attack.

He and his bride of three days left their honeymoon to be with his mother during this terrible time. They came to the memorial boards to post a picture of his father from happier times and a few words of memory.

The mother and the bride never said a word. However, their eyes and presence said it all. His mother was very appreciative of her son and his new wife. Not only for being there to support her, but also for the sacrifice the newlyweds had made by leaving their honeymoon to deal with the effects of this disaster.

All I could think of was how his bride must have loved this man very deeply. She too had ended her honeymoon to support her husband's loss due to this tragic moment in history.

The son said he hoped his father was finally at peace.

Not only did the family grieve the loss of their loved one, but they were also able to put to rest the

very difficult year of loving an individual who suffered
from such deep depression.

The Father

I did not often see the same person over and
over again at the memorial boards, but I did notice a
father who came every day and spoke to the same
mental health worker at the Red Cross Center.

When I first saw him, he had his son's picture
chained to his chest by a set of small chains - the sort
that tethers a pen to the counter tops in banks and
post offices. The chains surrounded him, front and
back. As if to symbolically state that he was chained
to his grief.

I often saw him and the mental health worker
on the back steps to the portable classroom building.
They would be looking over the river at the smoke still
rising from the ruins of the World Trade Center. I
saw that same scene for almost a week.

The last time I saw him was the day before my
assignment was over. He and the mental health
worker were standing on the ground, not on the steps
in back of the portable classroom. They faced the
river and the World Trade Center site. This time his
chains and the picture were gone. I can only guess
that he had worked through the grief. That on this
day he had come to a point where he could start to let
go and begin to accept the reality of his loss.

Life Disrupted

A sous-chef who worked at the *Windows of the World* – the restaurant at the top of the North Tower – came to the American Red Cross to see if they could help him replace his knives. He was not on duty when the planes hit, but he had left his knives there. Apparently, chefs buy and use their own knives at work. His were specially weighted for better handling and cost around $1,000. As this was an extra large expense for the Red Cross they had to get special permission to award him the money so he could continue his employment as a chef. Who would have thought a set of carving knives could keep you from employment?

One of the New Jersey State workers told me about a woman who came in to replace her driver's license. When the planes hit, she evacuated the building without her purse. Her purse held her money, her train ticket, her subway pass and the keys to her car and house. When she finally made it across the river, she could not even get into her car to drive the rest of the way home or get into her house. This was such a simple thing, but it was very important to daily routine.

Standing in front of the memorial boards, I had met the sister who was not willing to let go, regardless of the odds. The family who had been able to let go and found the peace they had struggled for; the peace that was more than just the death of a loved one.

And I witnessed the father who was finally able to let his son go.

In my short volunteer visit to this historic place and time, I saw people hold onto their grief, work through their grief, and come to acceptance with their grief.

Grief is a process. I liken it to a high tide and low tide; it is fluid. The goal is be in forgiveness and acceptance, or low tide. However, sometimes the high tide, or grief, sneaks up on us and reminds us we are vulnerable.

Lost – Part Three

The day I reported in at the Central Railroad of New Jersey Terminal, was also the day I had to change hotels. This was unfortunate as I knew how to get back to the Marriott, but had no idea how to get to the new hotel near the Secaucus Mall. Luckily, I thought Marti was staying at this hotel, along with all the other Red Cross workers. Marti didn't have a car, so I asked her to drive back with me, thinking she knew the way. After all, she'd done the route before, and she was used to heavy traffic being originally from Sothern California! I was wrong!

I will never understand how I, the small-town girl, always end up with the rental car and have to navigate in cities with their by-ways and turnpikes. Luckily for us we did not have to pay tolls (the Port Authority gave all American Red Cross cars a free pass on the Turnpike).

We got on the Turnpike without any problems. According to our directions we were to drive a certain distance and turn off on 'Exit B.' We came upon 'Exit B' quickly, perhaps too quickly. The sign said 'Hoboken.' Marti said, "We need Secaucus."

We quickly decided that we would get off at the exit. If it was wrong, how hard would it be to get back on?

We stopped at a grocery store near the end of the exit ramp, and we both asked different people how to get to Secaucus. My directions were via the Turnpike. Her directions were via the surface roads. She was the navigator, so we followed her directions.

We did not pay attention to the fact that it was around five o'clock in the evening and the middle of rush hour. Apparently not a good time for two lost out-of-staters to be driving in New Jersey.

We were on a four-lane highway with two lanes in each direction. It was bumper-to-bumper with slow, tight moving traffic. I just drove forward. I never changed lanes and hoped we would hurry up and come to our exit because the traffic was more than I was used to.

Yes, there it was the exit that we were told to get off on and we would be in Secaucus. So off we went, back onto the Turnpike. We stopped at the tollbooth and asked the attendant for more directions.

She said we just left the exit we were looking for. We should not have gotten on the Turnpike! She told us to go down to the end of the barrier, take a left and go to the other side, (apparently not a legal move on the Turnpike). We were to get off the Turnpike at the same exit we got on the Turnpike. So we did. We stopped at the tollbooth on the other side, now for the third time, explained our mistake and took off for Secaucus and finally found the hotel.

Before we left the Family Assistance Center, we agreed that the next morning all four of us would meet up at breakfast so we could drive together to the Railroad Terminal. Surprisingly they all knew the way back to the center and I didn't get lost.

The Holland Tunnel was closed because it emerged near the Ground Zero site. Consequently, the traffic was light by New Jersey standards which were just fine by my Montana standards! I memorized the route on my own and was OK from then on.

Adam Again

The first day at the Family Assistance Center did not involve a ferry ride. So when lunchtime came around I headed over to The Salvation Army food tent to meet up with my team and report on the morning events. Over the noise of the conversation and everyone getting food, I heard a very familiar voice. It was Adam.

Remember Adam from the airport? He was the one who introduced me to all the drivers. Adam was one of the food servers. "Maureen" he called out. He gave me a big hug, told me how happy he was to see me, and then introduced me to everybody in the food line. I was so happy to see him. Adam's presence was like a shining star to me, he would never understand how important he would become to me.

Debriefing

As team leader, I was required to report to a central meeting at the end of the day for a debriefing and briefing for the next day. We discussed what was happening at the Family Assistance Center, the ferry trips over to Ground Zero, and any changes in personnel.

In the middle of my stay, the American Red Cross personnel changed. Our center administrator and direct coordinator were rotated out and went home. It was hard because we had really enjoyed those people. They were good at running interference when the three volunteer agencies helping families had disagreements.

After one debriefing, I was asked by a N.O.V.A. worker to wait so she could talk to me. My team was being singled out for being a little too friendly. Apparently, N.O.V.A. was not accustomed to these friendly, outgoing social workers. They complimented me on my reserve, and said that was what they liked. I was reserved because I was the leader and had to keep an eye on my team. I just wandered round and talked to people. N.O.V.A. liked that, and they wanted me to temper back my team.

Apparently, my group of social workers was too outgoing. However, I never had that conversation with my team because I was pleased with their social worker skills. They were great, just the way they were, and I know the people they talked to really benefited from their particular kind of friendliness.

Chapter Five

My Special Moments

Ghosts of the Past

One time when I was just walking around the Railroad Terminal, I went back to and walked through the train shed. This was when I really noticed the memorial boards. These three-sided, six-foot high by three-foot wide cork boards were filled with pictures of missing loved ones, prayers and poems. I wasn't aware at the time that these boards were going to be a big part of my time and attention at the Terminal.

The Central Railroad of New Jersey Terminal in Liberty State Park happened to be more than just a train station; it was a transportation exchange for bus, ferry, commuter trains and long distance trains. The Statue of Liberty greeted the immigrants as they arrived in America. Ellis Island was the first

American soil they walked on and the Central Railroad of New Jersey Terminal was their ticket to their American Dream.

There was hope here. One day I just I closed my eyes and imagined the voices in multiple languages. Children laughing and crying, adults quiet and reserved as they took in their new surroundings.

I was standing in the same place where they had once stood themselves. I could hear the concentrated action and emotion that went on as trains arrived and passengers boarded or got off. I could sense the hope and adventure in these new Americans as their trains pulled out for places far away.

This train station took them to their future. Some stayed in the New York, New Jersey area, some traveled to other states where they had families. Some were the first of their family to come to America, leading the way for the other family members. This was the Promised Land. This was the land of opportunity and prosperity. If you were willing to work you could have your dream. A new life. A better life.

This was an intentional moment for me as I stopped and listened. I thought to myself, did my relatives walk through these gates? Perhaps my Irish relatives did. My Scottish relatives came through Canada. Perhaps my German, Bohemian or Danish contributions passed over this same spot.

My husband's grandparents came from Norway. They could have walked through these gates on their way to America's heartland.

New York City belongs to the world and the world walked through these gates. Our country's history walked through these gates once. This terminal contributed to my personal ancestry. These gates brought a new way of life to the many who sought the 'opportunity' of America.

Today I was standing on this train station's platform because the world was damaged by an act of terrorism.

I was now a part of that moment in time.

I stood on the history that built America.

And now I am standing on the history that will once again change America.

A One-Month Remembrance

Thursday, October 11th marked the end of the first month of this on-going tragedy. The Salvation Army held an interfaith remembrance service to acknowledge this date. There were two services and I went to the early morning one at 8:30 a.m.

It was foggy that morning and the air was heavy with the smell of the collapsed buildings; a combination of fire, cement, ash and tragedy. I'd been in two residence fires in my lifetime, and knew the distinct smell of fire. But this smell was different. It had its own unique smell. One I'll never forget.

Like the smell in the air and the fog that surrounded us I will not likely forget the words the minister spoke that morning.

"The steadfast love of the Lord never ceases, his mercies never come to any end; they are new every morning;..." Lamentations 3:22-23

"So we do not lose heart,"..."For we know that if the earthly tent we live in is destroyed, we have a building from God..." 2 Corinthians 4:16 and 5:1

Or the adaptation of the poem *We Remember* written by Rabbi Sylvan Kamens in the 1960's and published in 1970 in "New Prayers For the High Holy Days."

This same poem was presented at a memorial to those who lost their lives December 21, 1988 when a terrorist bomb exploded on Pam Am Flight 103 over Lockerbie, Scotland.

In the rising of the sun and in its going down,
We will remember them.
In the laughter of the past, and the tears of today
We will remember you.
In the opening of buds and in the rebirth of spring,
We will remember those who are no longer with us.

*In the blueness of the sky and in the warmth of
summer
In the flow of the river and the river of people
We will remember you.
In the rustling of leaves and the beauty of
autumn
In the briskness of fall and the chills of the
evening
We will remember those whom once were here.
In the beginning of yet another year and when it
comes to an end,
We will remember.
When we are weary and in need of strength,
We will remember those we knew and loved.
When we are lost and sick at heart,
We will remember.
When we have joys we yearn to share,
We will remember each one.
For as long as we live,
They too shall live
For they are now a part of us
As today, we promise that we will never forget.*

We ended the poignant service singing "God Bless America."

As our voices sang out "God Bless America, My home sweet home" the sun started to peek out through the fog, the gray lifted and once again the sky turned into a beautiful sunny day.

Chapter Six

The Journey to Ground Zero

The Families Gather at the Train Terminal

My Red Cross Disaster Mental Health team's main assignment was escorting family members to the site of The World Trade Center collapse, or Ground Zero as the media now called it. Our first trip over was on October 9, 2001. This will be a day that I will always remember.

For non-emergency workers, escorted ferry trips were the only opportunity to get to Ground Zero. The New Jersey Family Assistance Center had escorted trips from the Railroad Terminal and so did the New York Family Assistance Center from Pier 94 on Manhattan's west side. However, one had to be a family member of one of the victims, or a member of the support agencies like N.O.V.A., The Salvation Army, or the American Red Disaster Mental Health Team.

Family members had to preregister for this trip. They arrived on their assigned day, checked into the Family Assistance Center, and received a pass, a green badge. Then the families gathered in the main waiting room of the Railroad Terminal for the buses that would take them to the ferry. While the families waited in the large open terminal, the support workers used this time to mingle amongst them. It was an opportunity to get to know the families and let them know that we were there to offer any kind of support they needed - whether it be physical, spiritual, or just a friendly ear to listen.

The support staff wore numbered yellow badges with that day's date on them. We were asked to wear them above our nametags. These colored badges were the tickets we used to get on one of the four buses and the Hudson River ferry to Ground Zero and back.

I found myself disappointed during one trip that curiosity seekers managed to talk their way into a yellow badge just so they could experience Ground Zero. I know that this happens; I just felt it shorted the families of the support they could have used.

On one or our trips over I talked to an individual from a state agency. He wanted the opportunity to see the site so he asked for a badge to make the trip. He was not qualified to offer support to the families. The families were instructed that those with the yellow badges were there to be a support system on their journey to see Ground Zero.

This was just one of those moments when my innocence was bruised. I still wanted to believe the world was full of good and selflessness.

Getting Across the Hudson River

I will probably never forget the first trip over to Ground Zero. I was informed that this weather was typical for an October day in New York. It was a sunny day with a bright blue sky. There was a slight chill in the air and small breeze, just perfect for a ferry ride. Ever since I arrived, the weather had been great. Surprisingly, every day had been sunny, warm and cloudless. I guess I was expecting more fall weather, including some rain.

There were four buses waiting for us outside the Terminal. Marti, Dora, Rita and I each got on a different bus. I ended up on the fourth and last bus. Liberty Harbor Marina was a short distance away as the crow flies, but we had to drive up one side of the Morris Canal, cross over on the bridge and come down the other side to the marina.

As we were driving into the marina, I couldn't help but overhear two New Jersey Episcopal priests sitting behind me. They were reminiscing about how they had watched the construction of the World Trade

Center. They saw it grow taller and taller, reaching up into the sky. One priest remarked in a melancholy tone, "Seven years to build and an hour and half to destroy."

New York City

We had a small wait before we boarded at Liberty Harbor Marina. Finally we were all safely onboard the ferry and headed across the Hudson. On the New York side we docked at the World Financial Center ferry slip near the New York Mercantile Exchange.

The closer we got, the taller the buildings seemed to get. *They are so tall!* That's all I thought when I saw the World Financial Center buildings. Like the typical tourist, all I could do was look up. Everywhere I stared was tall buildings. I wasn't used to seeing that kind of height in something man-made.

As we were leaving the ferry, The Salvation Army handed out carnations to everyone so we could place them at the memorial that was set-up near the Ground Zero site.

Before leaving the ferry slip, we were instructed that the Ground Zero site was an ongoing crime scene. We were warned not to pick anything up, not to bend over, or in any way act suspiciously. Clutching our carnations, we set off through the World Financial Plaza. It was very quiet, and the silence took me by surprise. Following a path outlined by orange traffic cones, we walked through the plaza occasionally crossing temporary footbridges placed over very large electrical cables on the ground.

We walked en masse, moving silently. For just one moment, my team and I were one with these families.

When I looked up, I noticed several construction workers looking down on us. They were standing at attention with their hard hats over their chests. These men were paying tribute to the family members. They were offering their respect as the families made their sad pilgrimage to the site where their loved ones had died in this terrible tragedy. The sight of these men acknowledging these families with such respect brought tears to my eyes.

This silent salute and showing of respect was one of the softer sides of this tragedy that I witnessed during my visits to Ground Zero.

I kept looking around so I could take in all of this sight. It was surreal. Up beyond the construction workers and above the Securities and Exchange Building, about sixteen to twenty stories up, was a piece of the Twin Towers impaled in Three World Financial Center.

I grew up in the Midwest and was familiar with the power of a tornado. They could pick up pieces of debris and impale them into telephone poles or other solid masses. But this huge piece of metal sticking out of a building twenty stories high was something I couldn't imagine possible.

The massive impact of the explosion of the planes hitting the Towers, or the force of the Towers collapsing had thrown a piece of one building into the side of another building with unimaginable force. The building piece hung there like a splinter needing to be removed.

Feeling overwhelmed and small was apparently going to be my pattern on this journey. I consciously had to stop myself, recover my composure and continue walking. To my right, I noticed a golf cart on a small road next to our footpath. A New York police officer was at the wheel of this small vehicle. Next to him was an elderly woman.

The officer was clean-shaven and bald. His eyes were covered with black, rimless sunglasses. His large, muscular arms appeared to fill all of his shirtsleeves. He sat up straight, both hands on the wheel, staring straight ahead, silent and stoic. He seemed disconnected from his sad passenger as she was on her way to pay respects to her loved one.

Coming Upon Ground Zero

In our orientation for this trip we had been warned repeatedly that this was a crime scene and to stay on the basic route we were instructed to follow.

We were told that everything would be covered in gray or perhaps no color at all. I thought I understood what they meant. I had even fixed an image in my mind.

In the original *Wizard of Oz* movie the first part is in black and white. When the house lands on the witch and she is killed, Dorothy opens the door. At this point everything reverts to color. Except, in this scene everything was the opposite. We started out in color – blue skies, green trees and beige colored buildings. Suddenly it went to gray, or perhaps more like colorless.

I continued to be surprised by the sights I saw as we walked silently along.

Still moving en masse, our group walked past the North Cove Marina empty of the luxury yachts that were harbored there on September 11th. We walked past the shattered glass that covered The Winter Garden, now filled with broken palm trees. We quietly made our way toward Ground Zero. I wasn't sure where we were going so I just flowed with the crowd.

We came to a small park with trees still standing and started to see different signs of life. There was a Salvation Army mobile food distribution trailer with a food stand and tables, portable toilets and an area to rest and wash up.

Initially I found this very disorienting. We'd gone from a silent, contemplative walk through a deserted walkway and buildings to the hum of people talking and shouting, trucks revving up, backhoes beeping – all sounds of recovery. I looked up and saw a road sign – Liberty Street.

We walked along Liberty Street toward West Street, avoiding the fire trucks and semis that lined the opposite side. The World Trade Center site is bound by Liberty Street to the south and West Street to the west, Vesey to the North and Church Street to the East. We only got as far as the corner of Liberty Street and the Hudson River Greenway, which runs west of, and parallel to, West Street. Our destination was a set of wooden steps up to a viewing platform erected for visiting dignitaries; including the President of the United States and the Mayor of New York.

Before walking under the skywalk that led to the platform, I saw something that made me wish I had a camera. This sight has never left me. Standing against the gray wall of a building was a bright splash of color, a stack of orange and white five-gallon buckets, perhaps ten high and twenty across.

I had seen these buckets before on TV, immediately after September 11th. Rescue workers were using them for the delicate task of sifting through the debris for anything that could help with the rescue or identification of the victims. They were used like a fireman's water brigade, except in reverse. Empty buckets were passed from hand to hand over the twisted beams and broken concrete. Full buckets were passed back for examination and preservation. Silently, like centurions, these instruments of rescue were standing in formation waiting to be called upon to help again.

To this day a stack of orange and white five-gallon buckets makes me catch my breath.

The View From the Platform

As we walked under the skywalk, the sounds of rescue got louder and the dirt got grayer and muddy. We funneled up the wooden stairs to the platform that stood two stories high above the activity below. I brought up the rear. As I got on the platform I looked around in amazement. I struggled to comprehend what I was looking at.

All I saw was a colorless, senseless, chaotic mass. Backhoes and dump trucks moved backward and forwards in an attempt to pick up the debris and haul it off. Large semis were carrying off long and short I-beams of what I can only assume were the structure of the Towers. Occasionally a flame would pop through the debris. Smoke rose all around.

Even though I had never personally seen the World Trade Center Towers while they were standing, I could still recognize the style of the building. The tall narrow window facades that wrapped the building appeared like sheets of aluminum siding that were dropped and sticking out of the ground. They looked as delicate and airy as they did in pictures I had seen before I came. They were like headstones in a small cemetery on a gray, foggy morning.

Later that evening when I called home to talk to my husband, I did my best to describe the scene to him. I said it was as if you were on a beach and saw a wooden sand/snow fence, half-fallen down and leaning drunkenly against a beach hut. There in the colorless sand a child played with his matchbox-sized yellow Tonka truck – picking up sticks and sand and moving among the tall, broken wood fence stakes. It was surreal.

Around the perimeter of Ground Zero were the tall buildings of lower Manhattan. Those closest to the site were draped in large black net drop cloths – ten, twenty, thirty stories long. I had never seen anything like it before and it would take me a while to understand what I was looking at. All I could see on this first visit was a mountain of gray concrete and steel, surrounded by black shrouded buildings – like mourners looking on a gravesite.

Our Job

But...my job was not to gawk at this scene, my job was to be supportive and help the families come to terms with what they were seeing. Help them understand the incomprehensible.

The tone on the platform was hushed. Everyone stood there with a sense of reverence. People talked in whispers as if not to disturb the noise of the recovery workers. People would point to something shyly, as if they were afraid that they would get caught doing something bad and be punished.

On our second trip, Marti stood next to a woman who suddenly sank to the ground. Marti went right down with her. The woman quietly told her that she just wanted to pray. Marti stayed there with her to comfort her. I noticed this and quietly walked over to Marti and laid my hand on her shoulder. I just wanted her to know I too was there to support her, as she supported this woman.

On another visit, a family that appeared to be Muslim was coming to the site where their son's physical body was last seen on this earth. He was one of the several dozen innocent Muslims killed in the attack. They came to observe, experience, and pray as many other families had come to do.

I was touched to see that everyone on the platform recognized that this family had gathered close together and were softly talking. The observation platform full of other family members was respectful and gave them a little extra room and honored their privacy. They were there like all the other families to say their goodbyes to loved ones.

On the way back to the ferry, we stopped at a memorial site to leave our carnations and say a few words or think a silent prayer. On our way to Ground Zero I walked right past the memorial site without noticing it. I was probably so absorbed in my surroundings I missed it or did not recognize it. It was a huge pile of flowers and pictures of loved ones, teddy bears and posters. Multiple signs saying, "Have you seen me?" with a picture of a missing person and a name and telephone number of a grieving family member. With each visit the memorial seemed to get bigger and bigger.

On my last trip to Ground Zero I recognized the same New York policeman I saw on the first trip. He was still driving a golf cart, transporting another elderly lady to view the scene of destruction. His arms were still too big for his shirtsleeves. However, this time his sunglasses were propped on his forehead and he steered the golf cart with one hand. The other hand lay comfortingly on the shoulder of the older woman sitting next to him. He too had become softer, more understanding with each trip to the site.

Trying to Make Sense of It

By our last visit, I had found some form of context in which I could understand what I was looking at. The chaos and rubble began to take shape. The dust rolled around first obscuring the scene, then clearing, like fog on the ocean.

I could see the bottom four or five floors of the South Tower. I saw the corner posts and the high arches that ringed the base of the Tower. It was haunting to see those once strong upward lines of the Tower now blackened ghostly skeletons against the gray. I had only seen the Twin Towers in photographs, standing tall and gleaming silver and white against a blue sky. Now I was seeing them in person, black and gray. I will always be haunted by that scene.

Despite the destruction the remains of the building still stood strong and powerful. Almost as if she was defying those who had tried to destroy her. It was almost as if the building was trying to say, "You have damaged me, but you have not destroyed me."

On our last trip back to the ferry, I seemed to have a better sense of what happened on those sixteen acres of debris. Although I knew no one in the buildings and didn't live in the New York area, I was bound to the tragic moment as if part of me was left at the scene.

Back to New Jersey

October 13th was my last ferry trip. On that day, as we were headed back to New Jersey, we picked up an escort. Two New York police boats accompanied us over to the New Jersey side. They hadn't been with us when we took the trip over, nor had they been there on any of the other previous trips. However, this time they were definitely with us and they were escorting us back to New Jersey. Someone on board said, "It must be due to the invasion of Afghanistan." The rest of the trip was in silence. I must have missed the actual invasion news (October 7, 2001) in the trauma and drama of our visits to Ground Zero, but the sight of the two armed police boats made it very clear - we were at war.

A True Friend - Adam

After each ferry trip, Adam would seek me out and ask me how it went. I would talk and he would listen. He asked questions and I answered. He would share with me any news or activities that happened at the Terminal that day. It was a relief to talk to him. Adam turned out to be my debriefer. I don't think he ever knew how important these talks were to me.

I attended the formal debriefings given by N.O.V.A. at the end of each day, but my talks with Adam were definitely more beneficial. Adam always seemed to be there for me. He was there when I arrived at Newark Airport. He was there when I arrived at the Family Assistance Center. He was there at the end of my volunteer days. Adam was a genuine, compassionate person, he was my hero; and he probably doesn't even know it.

Chapter Seven

Heading Home

It turned out that my last ferry trip was the last trip for everyone from the New Jersey Family Assistance Center across the Hudson River to Ground Zero.

Our last ride back was quiet. The only noise was the ferry engine and the roar of our police boat escort. Between the news that we were at war and the vision of Ground Zero, a quiet contemplative blanket fell over this last ferry trip.

We silently got on the buses and returned to the Terminal. As quiet as the last trip was, the families seemed to disperse just as quietly to their cars and back to the new normality of their lives without their loved ones.

Airlines – Part One

I was saddened at the thought of leaving, but excited about going home. The past two weeks had been so packed with different sights, sounds and emotions; each experience seemed to have gone on forever. Even though I had adjusted to all the tall buildings and congested living environment, home and the fresh mountain air called me back; and I was ready to go.

Delta Airlines wasn't ready for me!

Delta was not aware that Red Cross Disaster Mental Health Workers were only required to work two weeks. All other Red Cross volunteers worked three weeks. My local Red Cross had made my travel arrangements, they should have known about the two weeks.

When I called Delta to confirm my flight home, they gave me a date that was one week away from my expected departure date. This wasn't acceptable. I needed to get home to Great Falls, to my husband, my friends and my clients. I had anticipated flying out on October 14th.

Delta said, "Sorry, all flights are full, how about the 15th?" I said, "No, you don't understand, I have to leave on October 14th." It took some time and a couple of phone calls over a three-day period before Delta finally found me a seat.

I wasn't going to return through Minneapolis, my preferred route. I was going to go back through

Salt Lake City.   However, that was still better than flying to Seattle and then flying back to Great Falls.

Goodbyes

With my flight time secured, I was able to start my goodbyes. I looked for my team members so we could arrange a time to head back to the hotel. This was also their last day. Marti and Rita were ready to go home, but Dora was busy counseling a bereaved family. We decided we would walk around and say our goodbyes to the people who had been our 'family' for two weeks.

My first stop was the 'end of the day' debriefing.   It was at this debriefing that they announced that today was the last ferry trip from the Family Assistance Center. There would be no more sorrowful ferry loads of grieving families that would cross the river to Ground Zero. They also announced that the Family Assistance Center was gearing down and getting ready to close.

My next stop was to walk around the Terminal one last time so I could capture in my mind the amazing interior. I wanted to burn the image of that magnificent building into my mind. As cameras were not allowed, I wanted one final view so I could sear the memory into my brain.

Again I looked around at the glazed brick walls.   The intricate red iron trusses soared above holding up the cathedral roof, three-stories above me. I stared at the huge staircase leading to the bricked up view of the Hudson. Maybe one day they'd uncover the windows and the world would gaze across the river to the site of so much sorrow and loss.

I walked out the back door to the portable classrooms. The once fresh green new turf was now trodden down and dried up. The weather had allowed for those beautiful blue cloudless days. However that also meant no rain since September 11th. It had been over a month of dry, cloudless, sunny, beautiful days. The only moisture in this part of the world was from the tears of the living.

My goodbyes to the other American Red Cross mental health workers would have to wait until that night at the hotel, as they were all busy with families.

Memory Boards

Walking back through the old train shed, I stopped again at the cork Memory Boards. I read them for what must have been the hundredth time. All those messages of hope and despair left there.

I wanted to leave my own note on the boards. I wanted a bit of me to stay here near Ground Zero. I wanted to thank the families who posted their thoughts, prayers and wishes on these boards for all to read. I wanted to wish them strength and courage in the days to come. And I wanted them to know how humbled I was to be part of this experience. I didn't leave my name, I simply signed it an American Red Cross Volunteer.

Here is what I wrote...

As I wander amongst these Memory Boards
I can't help butt to be humbled and awed.

By the senselessness of your loss . . .
The depth of your grief . . .
And the strength of your ability to heal.

A part of me remains here with you,
Because I have been . . .
forever changed by having met you.

An American Red Cross Worker

I stood back and stared at the boards through my tears. My time here was more, so much more, that just any volunteer experience. In my time here I witnessed the enormity of the disaster and the human tragedy. It had turned from a national tragedy into a personal one.

Taking a deep breath and wiping away my tears, I moved on through the train shed and stood by a gate leading to one of the abandoned railroad tracks. I closed my eyes, just as I did the week before.

I imagined the hustle and bustle of the departing trains that bore the immigrants who crossed this threshold on their way to their American dream. Mixed in with the noise of the workers at the Family Center, I imagined I could hear our ancestors' long-gone voices, shouting, crying, laughing and praying as they set out on their adventures.

Farewell To Adam

With one reluctant backwards look, I moved into The Salvation Army food tent to find Adam. This was going to be one sad 'goodbye.' Adam was all excited and wanted to tell me all about his day off yesterday. Back in Indiana, he'd done some research and secured two interviews at New York universities, and yesterday was the day for them. Adam wanted to return to the Big Apple and make it his home.

I shared with Adam that it was time for me to leave. In Adam fashion he announced to everyone that I was leaving. I wasn't allowed to sneak out. Adam had me say goodbye to everyone Adam had introduced me to such a short time ago. It was very emotional; we had all been through so much together. Then, with one last big hug for Adam, I had to leave.

God speed Adam in all your adventures – you deserve the best.

Last Thoughts

I moved outside to the walkway by the Hudson River. It was here on that fateful September day the Central Railroad of New Jersey maintenance workers heard and saw the first plane hit the World Trade

Center. I looked across the river to where I imagined the Twin Towers soared over the city.

I'd never seen them in person, but their picture was fresh in my mind. Smoke no longer rose from the site, and unless you knew exactly where the Towers stood, it was difficult to see the hole in the skyline. I stopped to burn one last image into my memory; Manhattan without the famed outline of the World Trade Center Towers.

I'd been in New Jersey for two weeks. I had come not as a visitor, but as a volunteer. I lost no one. I knew no one. Yet that day, September 11, 2001, would change my life forever.

I met ordinary people who'd had an extraordinary experience.

I had two weeks of just listening, not talking. I heard one story after the other. They spoke of the same event, but never the same story. I found myself inside the heads of people, witnessing human struggle, strength, and vulnerability.

I met good and evil on my journey to a place called Ground Zero. I tried to make sense of the senselessness when I stood on the viewing platform at Ground Zero looking out at the surrounding devastation.

September 11th would become a moment in history that would never go away; like Pearl Harbor, it was frozen in time. The event would change us and permanently affect the future.

But now it was time for me to go.

I turned to the right to say farewell to Ellis Island and the Statue of Liberty. Lady Liberty stood there silently guarding the harbor that had greeted my ancestors as they traveled to this great country.

At the arranged time I picked up Dora, Rita and Marti, and we drove away from Liberty State Park for the last time. Our farewell dinner was at our favorite Italian restaurant in the Secaucus Mall.

I had my usual – fresh mozzarella rolled in prosciutto, then rolled again in some Italian green leaf, bathed in a warm bath of a balsamic vinegar reduction. This will always be my New Jersey meal. I've tried to re-create that meal many times, with no success. It will join my other favorite life memories.

While backpacking through Europe one summer I had the best cup of coffee I can remember. It was at a youth hostel in Normandy, France. A strong, hot cup of coffee served in a glass bowl with warm cream. Another food moment in time I will not be able to recreate.

Lost – For the Last Time

October 14th and we were homeward bound. Marti and Rita were also flying home from Newark Airport around the same time. Dora was going to drive home to Florida. We all drove together to the Red Cross Administrative Center. Although we were eager to all head home, I believe we were reluctant to part company and wanted to extend our time together.

The Administrative Center had moved from the college campus where I'd checked in two weeks ago. It was now in an empty warehouse in some industrial zone. No one was more surprised than I that we made it there from the hotel without getting lost. It must have been the excellent directions, or that my luck had changed and I wasn't directionally challenged anymore!

Our good luck didn't last too long. We'd arranged for a car and driver to meet us at the Administrative Center to take us to the airport. This professional driver found the warehouse without any problem, and we all piled in with our luggage.

For the first time in two weeks, I was able to sit back and let someone else do the driving. Out of habit I asked for directions to Newark Airport. I always like to know where I'm going. The driver wouldn't share his directions with me. He assured us that he knew how to get there. Traffic was getting heavier at that time of the day, but we weren't worried. After all, he was a professional driver and knew how much time was needed to get to the airport at that time of day. He probably also knew how to get there in the easiest and shortest way.

We were wrong to trust him.

He got stuck in the left-hand lane of bumper-to-bumper traffic when he needed to be in the right-hand lane to take the needed exit. I saw the sign to the airport and told the driver he should move over, but he didn't believe me and we missed the exit. He was lost and didn't know what to do. I called his dispatcher to get a new route.

I must admit it did feel good to know that I, the out-of-stater, was not lost, but the New Jersey native, and professional driver, was very lost! Luckily the driver had only to go to the Delta terminal, so we avoided the time consuming and confusing loops around Newark Airport. We eventually made it with enough time to check our bags and say our sad goodbyes before heading out to catch our respective planes.

Airlines – Part Two

Marti and Rita sailed through baggage check-in. With my flight mix-up, I didn't have a paper ticket. I gave the counter check-in person my identification and told her my flight number. She found my reservation easily enough. She then called over her supervisor. I was told to follow the supervisor to an X-ray machine. I didn't really have a choice. I needed the flight home and she had my ID and ticket in her hand. So I followed her over to an X-ray machine.

This was not normal procedure pre 9-11. This may be normal for today's traveler, but back then, it meant something was wrong. Before September 11th, you could go from the curbside drop off to the flight gate with only one quick check of your boarding pass at the gate. No luggage scans, no body scans, nothing in those securities-less days before someone figured out how to turn airplanes into bombs.

Both my suitcase and backpack were X-rayed and I was given a full body pat down. I did not expect this and was very uncomfortable. They gave me my backpack, identification, ticket, gate number, and told me I would have to check in again at the gate.

By now I was upset and wondering what had happened that I was singled out. I reoriented myself, found the concourse and set off for my gate. With my luck, it would be at the farthest end of a very long concourse. As it was!

When I got to the gate I didn't rush right up to the counter. I lingered to see what other people were doing. Everything seemed fine. People were going up to the counter, talking to the agent and walking away. I thought, *OK, no problem here.* I went up to the counter, told the agent my name and handed over my ID and ticket, just like all the other people.

She asked for my backpack.

This was definitely not what I'd seen happen to the others. Since I just wanted to get home, I gave it to her. She then asked my permission to open it and search through it. I reluctantly gave her permission.

She thoroughly searched through my possessions, then said, "Thank you Miss McInnis, here's your ID and ticket. I need to keep your backpack. You will get it back when you board."

Needless to say I was not happy. My purse with all my money was in that backpack. The agent wasn't interested in my protests and said again, "You'll get it back when you board."

I watched her place it next to three or four other pieces of carry-on luggage near the walkway door. At least I wasn't the only one singled out for this special attention. I didn't travel very far from that door; I wanted to have my possessions in my sight at all times. Anyway, I didn't have any money to get anything, so I just waited.

Soon enough my flight was called and I got in line to board. My backpack was handed to me and they wished me a good flight. And it was a good flight. It was quiet.

Airlines – Part Three

At Salt Lake City I checked my connection and went to the gate to wait. About ten minutes before the flight boarded I heard my name called asking me to go to the gate counter. I went up, introduced myself and said, "You paged me?" "Yes," the agent said, "may I see your ID, ticket and backpack please?"

I must have dropped my jaw in astonishment because she repeated the request. Again, reluctantly, I handed over my possessions. And, again, they searched and placed my backpack by the gate. And, again, I got it back as I boarded.

As I look back on what happened it made sense that during that time period, while I was flying out of the Newark Airport, changing your flight three times and insisting on traveling on a particular day could be a red flag to the airlines. I had a reservation for a period of time and then in the last few days I called the airlines and demanded to change it. In fact, I changed my reservation to and from Newark International Airport three times in a ten-day period. Not a good idea in that post 9-11 period when our nation was recovering from terrorist attacks and in the process of invading another country.

Needless to say I was very glad to see the lights of Great Falls appear below my plane, and never happier to be home.

Chapter Eight

Ten Years
Looking Back

First Anniversary

On the first anniversary of 9-11, the Great Falls Fire Department held a ceremony outside of their main department firehouse commemorating the deaths of the 343 firefighters and paramedics who died in the collapse of the World Trade Center Towers. It was a very moving tribute with both the Fire Chief and Mayor of Great Falls speaking about the bravery and tragic losses on that day. Each time a name was called out, a brass bell was rung; the traditional symbol for remembering firemen.

I went to this ceremony for two reasons. The first reason was my ongoing involvement with the Great Falls Fire Department. I volunteered with the Juvenile Fire Setter Program and the American Red Cross Response Team.

The second reason was I wanted to be in a place where I could reflect and remember my time at Ground Zero. I may not have been able to completely relate to the loss of a fellow fireman, however, I did understand the reality of the tragedy from a human perspective.

Many of the emotions I experience and memories that I still held onto were stirred up that day. I happened to notice that of the three Great Falls mental health workers who volunteered for the Red Cross at Ground Zero, I was the only one at this ceremony. The other two disaster workers had been assigned to Pier 94 in Manhattan. I was not actually aware of who had gone to New York until I met them in Great Falls at a post volunteer debriefing.

I had tried recruiting mental health workers to volunteer when I returned from my experience. After my two-week volunteer assignment at the New Jersey Family Assistance Center, I was so excited I thought I would share that experience. I told the other mental health counselors about it at the monthly Great Falls Counselors Association meeting. After that meeting, a social worked called the Red Cross and volunteered her time. She was one of the two Great Falls counselors at Pier 94 in Manhattan.

After the First Anniversary ceremony I stopped by to talk to the Fire Marshal and his assistant. These were the two firemen with whom I worked in the Juvenile Fire Setter program. We talked about my volunteer time in New York. I shared with them that on my day off one of my fellow mental health workers and I went into the City and took a Gray Line double-decker bus tour through Manhattan, traveling as far north as Harlem. After the tour, we walked around and came upon a fire station with a couple of firemen hanging around just inside the open double doors. My fellow disaster mental health worker introduced herself as the mother of a San Diego fireman. We told them of our mission and how sorry we were for the loss of so many of their fellow firemen - it was a moving moment.

That same fall, the Great Falls Fire Department sponsored a hunting trip in the Rocky Mountains for some New York City firemen from Ladder Company 12 and Ladder Company 25. I asked the Fire Marshal to get the New York firemen to sign the inside of the New York Fire Department baseball cap I had picked up while in New York.

I had bought this specific cap so I had a place to put all my pins. I had collected an American Red Cross 9-11 Team pin, two of the New Jersey Central Railroad Terminal pins that our team wore and my 9-11 pin I bought with a donation. These items are my only tangible mementos of my time at Ground Zero.

Second Anniversary

Malmstrom Air Force Base is stationed in Great Falls. For their 9-11 second anniversary I was asked to speak at their ceremony.

The Medical Flight Pharmacy Team was in charge of organizing this ceremony. They wanted someone who had been working at Ground Zero, preferably a mental health worker. So they called the local American Red Cross and asked if there were any mental health workers in Great Falls that had worked in New York during this time. They called me first and I was more than happy to do the talk.

So there I was on September 11, 2003, the guest speaker at the Malmstrom Air Force Base 9-11 Second Anniversary Commemoration. Writing the speech was hard. I was told that they wanted something that was upbeat and hopeful. That got me to thinking about the healing I saw during my volunteer assignment. I tried to make every thought poignant. My eyes must have filled with tears at nearly every other thought.

Eventually I was able to get the speech written and delivered it without breaking down. I talked of my experiences with the Port Authority of New York and New Jersey while at the Marriott Hotel. I talked of experiences with families at the New Jersey Family Assistance Center and the ferry trips across the Hudson River to Ground Zero. I told them about the people I had met who had lost loved ones and found hope with the assistance of the American Red Cross and the many other volunteers.

At the end of my speech the Base Commander came up to thank me. When I shook hands with him, he discreetly pressed a Malmstrom Air Force coin into my palm. He held my hand with both his hands, thanked me for my talk and service during that tragic time in our history, and explained to me the coin he had just given me.

Later at a quiet moment I read the inscription:

341st Space Wing One
Pax Orbis Per Arma Aeria
(World Peace Through Air Strength)

One Team, One Family, One Fight.

9-11 Impact on My Family

In 2002, my husband's oldest son joined the Army. Not out of some patriotic duty, but out of survival. He was not really prepared to be on his own with any success. The Army at least offered him employment, housing and meals.

David's training took many turns before he finally ended up on a Stryker Brigade Combat Team out of Fort Lewis, Washington. Fortunately, he was only twelve hours away from us here in Montana. When he had leave he would came back to Montana. Sometimes he would bring his friends back with him. This made his father very happy, as he was able to continue to see his son and be part of his life even while he was in the military.

November 14, 2003, David was deployed with the Iraqi Freedom Campaign for his first tour. They were sent to Baghdad. One year and one Purple Heart later he returned from deployment. He and his team all earned their Purple Hearts for their injuries when their Stryker was hit by an I.E.D. (an improvised explosive device). Fortunately their injuries were not fatal. Mostly concussions and some cuts.

His father had spent that whole year worrying about David's safety. He supported him the best he could by sending packages of food, beef jerky, powdered Gatorade and baby wipes. He sent him whatever was requested.

Happiness in Time of War

When David returned to Fort Lewis after his first deployment, he met a young lady by chance in a bar one evening. She was not just any young lady; she was destined to be the future Mrs. David, his Army wife. We found Jessica to be an amazing individual. She was studying to be a kindergarten teacher and her patience was exactly what David needed. We had the pleasure of meeting Jessica on one of our annual trips to Washington when we visited Marti and her husband. David and Jessica drove over for lunch and we loved her from the start.

We were invited to meet her folks on one of our camping trips to the Washington beach. It turned out that her folks lived thirty miles away from one of our favorite Washington State Parks - Grayland Beach. On one of our previous trips to Grayland, we drove around the area just getting to know it. By coincidence, we had actually driven through Jessica's hometown.

Her family was known for their campfire pit and blazing fire. So on one of our trips, we stopped by late one afternoon to enjoy their fire and get to know them. We were instantly accepted with warm hugs and cold beers.

Jessica's family and close friends were just as amazing as Jessica was. We were welcomed into that family from the second we met them. John and Julie, Jessica's folks, felt that David and Jessica balanced each other well. Both were willing to do what the other liked to do. John and Julie had accepted David as their own son in a house full of daughters.

David and Jessica were married in April of 2006. David had been called up for a second deployment. They decided to marry before he was to take off for a year.

They were married on a rainy Saturday. It may have rained the whole day of the wedding but it didn't stop the ceremony from being beautiful. Both David and Jessica had written their own vows to each other. The wedding ceremony ended in dramatic dip and a loving kiss.

David's father and I were so fortunate to be able to share this weekend with this great new family David had married into.

Back to War

Kevin, David's only brother, joined the Army Reserves the year prior to David's marriage. His reserve unit had been called up for deployment earlier in 2006. The month before his brother's wedding, Kevin left for a one-year deployment in Iraq. He belonged to an Ordinance unit (ammunition). Although he was not directly in harm's way, he was still overseas and involved in the war. Kevin was another person for his father to worry about.

David's second deployment orders were for July of 2006. He still belonged to the Stryker team. Part of his job on this deployment was to 'kick down doors and search homes.' Again his father worried about his safety while he was gone.

With the second tour, Jessica's family took on the monthly campaign to send David a package. They had totally taken in David and loved him as if he was their own.

War Becomes Up Close and Personal

While on his second tour David befriended another staff sergeant from Fort Lewis doing basically the same job, but in a different squadron. Staff

Sergeant Darrell Griffin, Jr. He was known as 'Skip' to his family, but David called him 'Griff.'

Griff was well read and a philosopher. He and David would smoke cigars at day's end and talk philosophy. They had become close friends.

Griff was keeping a journal about how he was experiencing the war during this deployment. He was also writing to his father back in California. After his service, he was hoping to turn it into a book. He called his journal, "The Great Conversation." I liken this journal to Victor Frankl's *Man's Search for Meaning*. This book is not so much about the war itself, but the experience of being involved in war.

Staff Sergeant Darrell 'Skip' Griffin, Jr. - Griff to his war friends - died March 21, 2007, a sniper shot to the head. My stepson lost a great friend and fellow soldier. The War had now crossed a line; it had now gotten up-close and personal.

Griff didn't finish his book.

His father, Darrell Griffin, Sr. did.

Last Journey, A Father and Son in Wartime is the title. On the back cover John McCain, U.S. Senator and former P.O.W wrote this note; "*Last Journey* is a remarkable and very moving account of the loss of his son. A father's need to know how and why it happened and the relationship between the parent and child changed and deepened by war."

Griff died the week before David went on his two-week R&R. His Washington family took him in when he came home and surrounded him with the love that only a family can offer. There were cousins in this close-knit family who were EMTs and volunteer firemen. They sat with David around the famous campfire pit and spoke of their own experiences with loss and recovery. To this day David wears a black metal bracelet with Griff's name and all his information engraved on it. I can't say I've ever seen him take it off.

Our Family Grows

When Kevin was home on his two week R&R he married his fiancée. It was a small wedding and somewhat unexpected. His father and I were the only family members there.

Kevin missed his brother's wedding because he was already deployed. David missed his brother's wedding because he was still on his second deployment.

When David returned for his two week R&R, Kevin had already returned home from his deployment and was back to his civilian job. We all went out to Washington to spend time with David.

During this break, David and Jessica decided it would be a good time to start a family. David would be back before the baby was born, he would also be home during those younger months.

David's daughter, our first granddaughter, was born in December 2007. Although surrounded with her close-knit family, Jessica was alone for the first six months of her pregnancy. David made it home in

October to share the last three months and the birth of his first child.

David was called up for a third deployment. While in Iraq, he re-upped with the army. He did note that this tour was relatively quiet compared with the first two. When he re-upped, he requested to be in a non-deployable position. He wanted to be home more. Be with his family for a while and not off at war.

As of this writing, David and Jessica have been married a little over five years. Twenty-seven months of that they were separated with David gone on deployment. For a combined additional eighteen months; he was away training and preparing to go on the deployments. Jessica understood what it meant to be a military wife when she said, "I do." David is blessed with this amazing loving wife and amazing loving family in-law.

The Army made David a man, the war made David a patriot, but the loving family he married into made David whole.

Although I was the one who went to Ground Zero as a volunteer with the American Red Cross, my family and extended family have all been affected by the 9-11 tragedy.

The related wars have brought great sorrow - the loss of David's friend and peer, Griff and David's experience of being in a war zone.

It has also brought great joy. Both of the boys have married. And we have been extra blessed by

Jessica, her extended family and our first granddaughter.

Final Thoughts

In the last ten years I have written these words a million times in my head. I really needed to get those thoughts and experiences out of my head so I could move on. As you can see, I finally got serious and started putting these words on paper in April of 2011. It was finally ready to get the words, the thoughts, the experiences and feelings out of my head and onto paper.

On May 2nd, 2011, the *Great Falls Tribune* headline announced that Osama Bin Laden had been killed. Ten years in the making but that mission has been accomplished. Bin Laden was credited with the masterminding and funding of the attacks on 9-11 along with the World Trade Center bombing in 1993. Terrorism in America and other parts of the world will continue. But the death of Osama Bin Laden ends a chapter, and hopefully the book.

As I look back, I didn't intend for my two-week American Red Cross volunteer assignment to affect my life so deeply. It just seemed to take on a life of its own. It changed me, not in a big bold way, but in a deeper more personal way.

The World Trade Center was my last American Red Cross volunteer assignment in faraway places. With my return from the New Jersey Family

Assistance Center I have kept my volunteering close to home.

I worked a while longer with the American Red Cross locally helping with house fires. Then I worked with a local parenting organization teaching parenting classes and co-parenting classes to divorcing couples. I also added more pro bono work to my private mental health practice.

I was able to continue to help the Great Falls Fire Department with their Juvenile Fire Setting Program. I was even fortunate enough to be selected to go to the National Fire Academy in Emmetsburg, Maryland - the home of the National Firemen's Memorial. The names of all the firemen who died in the September 11th tragedy are inscribed there, along with the names of every American fireman who died in the line of duty. Every day on my way to class, I would stop at the memorial to remember.

Chapter Nine

MY CONFESSION

My desire to volunteer for this assignment was purely selfish.

I wanted to be a part of this historic moment. I wanted the experience of being one of the few volunteers that could say that they were there.

I wanted people to say "Wow! You were there? Tell me what it was like."

Was that so terrible? I was willing to give two weeks of my time, my family's time, and my client's time to volunteer and use my skills to help. I make a living exchanging my expertise for money. This was exchanging my expertise for the experience.

At first, I was disappointed that I was not assigned to Pier 94 in New York City.

That was until I got to the New Jersey center. I would not trade one day of that experience.

The Central Railroad of New Jersey, the journey to Ground Zero, and all the people I met; both volunteers and family members. Individually, and collectively, they changed me. They made me better.

Does that make me bad or self-centered?

Many people saw this day as an act of evil. Not just the World Trade Center Towers, but the hit on the Pentagon and intended hit on the White House.

While on assignment, I even heard someone ask, "How could God let this happen?"

God didn't 'let' this happen. Human beings made decisions based on beliefs and then this happened.

Is man basically good or evil? This is my favorite debate.

Can evil exist if good is not also present?

Maybe that is why I needed to go on this assignment.

In the movie *Starman*, by John Carpenter (1984), Jeff Bridges plays an alien. His spacecraft was shot down over northern Wisconsin. He clones the body of Karen Allen's recently deceased husband. He talks her into driving him to Arizona where his mothership will pick him up in three days. Of course he is being chased by the government agents who shot him down in the first place.

Along the way, he learns a lot about love, but more importantly, he learns about who we are as a race.

There is a funny scene in which Allen is taking a nap and Bridges is driving. She wakes up from her nap as he is approaching an intersection with a traffic light that is yellow. There is a semi-truck full of baled hay headed for the same intersection. Bridges starts to speed up. Allen starts yelling, "What are you doing?" After they pass through the intersection causing a three-car crash behind him, Bridges innocently says that he watched her drive very carefully. Red means "stop", green means "go" and the yellow light "go very fast."

At the end of the movie, they make it to Winslow, Arizona, safely and stop to get something to eat. It is here that the government agency and military catch up to them. The extra-terrestrial scientist the government hired wants to ask him so many questions.

Alien Bridges starts to share that we are a 'strange' group of people. He then states that we are also 'beautiful.'

The best statement is when he tells the agent what makes us beautiful. He says,
"You are at your very best when thing are worst."

For the last 26 years, I have never forgotten that statement.

I often think of it when a tragedy strikes and people gather together to help people they don't know. Like fund-raisers when people are sick or bagging sand when the rivers are flooding faster then people can move out. It doesn't matter if the tragedy is big or small that statement always seems to come to mind.

That is why I needed to go on this journey. When things were at their worst, we are at our best.

The passengers on the flight that crashed in Pennsylvania were at their best when things were at their worst.

The volunteers who came to New York and New Jersey, were they not at their best?

The rescue workers who rushed into those burning buildings, the recovery workers who worked 24 hours a day for months upon months, and all those New Yorkers that stood in long lines to donate blood - were they not at their best?

Someone said to me recently that the time following Tuesday morning, September 11, 2001, was the softer side of New York.

I would like to believe that this journey was me at my best.

That sense of awe and wonder by the bigness of the city, touched by how people I didn't know softened in front of me, and reaching out to people I will never see again and offering support and words of encouragement.

I want to continue to naïvely believe that all people have good in them.

I write this little story of my memories and experiences to remind me, and hopefully you, that life is a balance of good and evil.

I believe that evil is a choice, just as good is a choice. One cannot exist without the other.

Alan Jackson titled his song *"Where were you when the world stopped turning on that September day?"*

Perhaps a better title would have been:

'WHO were you on that September day when the world stopped turning?'